A Child's Sketch
of the Afterlife

poems by

Brian Dickson

Finishing Line Press
Georgetown, Kentucky

A Child's Sketch
of the Afterlife

ACKNOWLEDGMENTS

I gratefully acknowledge the editors of the following journals, in which the poems
listed below first appeared:

Back Room Poetry, playing deck edition: "Throwback Thursday"
New Feathers Anthology: "And the Turkey Leg Beats Ad Infinitum" and "Stockings"
Paddler Press: "Last Frost," "Drought," and "Hayfield"
Pinyon: "Indigenous Head in a Neighbor's Window"
Tipton Poetry Review: "Cabin Fever"

Special thanks to Jennifer Moore for her sound advice and time, and for my writing
group, the *Visceral Realists*, for your steady encouragement over the years we met.

Aurelio Madrid, friend and philosopher, also did the cover of my other chapbook
with FLP, *Maybe This is How Tides Work*. You can find his work at www.
aureliomadrid.com.

Some really rough drafts of these poems were inspired by Nate Ragolia's "captured
noun" photography. For more about him visit www.nateragolia.com.

Publisher: Leah Huete de Maines
Editor: Christen Kincaid
Cover Art: Aurelio Madrid
Author Photo: Jenna Duke
Cover Design: Elizabeth Maines McCleavy

Order online: www.finishinglinepress.com
also available on amazon.com

Author inquiries and mail orders:
Finishing Line Press
PO Box 1626
Georgetown, Kentucky 40324
USA

Contents

To Sarah and Sophia. Thank you for everything.

Apparition Site of the Virgin Mary

She appeared in white garb,
halo, no baby in tow,
in front of a humming
cylinder at the nuclear plant
where he worked.

Then the same vision
before his corn crop
at home—a glow in the rows.

How many ears spilling
from the light?
Madonnas nestling
in the husks?

His land now
this pecan grove, a small,
wooden shrine right
off the highway.

I am as thirsty
as the sky is
for a dark cloud—all
this yellow around
until further notice.

Indigenous Head in the Neighbor's Window

Oh! Sealed lips
with yucca fiber!

Where is Chaco Canyon?
Where are your three sisters?

The liquor store past lawns
with American flags on the rumps

of bronze fawns—
Do we share desire's

exhaust pipe?
Spring can't uncoil soon enough.

Ode to the Corpse Flower

Vishnu is
sleeping for the
millionth time
at the bottom
of the pot.

His navel sprouting
this spear-bloom—

Brahmin at the tip
kissing
another universe
into existence
with its infinite
rot-wisdom.

I would follow
you into
that
funk.

And the Turkey Leg Beats Ad Infinitum

My old self stuffed
in a boot
tucked in a turkey
bought from a local farm
with *natural open space,*

where I visited
natural open space,
where I fed it grain,
slept on a cot,
shot it the next morning.

What a joke of a jake,
my new self said
to my old self.

Come on pilgrim, my new-
ness said. *Let's make
progress with your soul,*
half-baked boot
ready to roll.

Cabin Fever

Four days below ten degrees,
and the three blind mice shuffled
in with their placards complaining
about the lack of pepper jack cheese.

We peer into their hole on their day off.
The butcher's wife on trial, chunks
of tails as evidence, her statement:
I'm innocent, your honors.

Damn furries have all the power,
their canes flailing, sunglasses askew,
their gibberish written in twine.
What can we do, love?

See how we run with gossip
to our neighbors, show
our trial sketches without
a glint of a blade.

Stockings

Forgive me
for embracing you
so late in life.

As a young Jehovah's Witness
you only existed
as sad things with holes, lump

of coal gleaming
from the bottom, pieces
to chalk doomed
sidewalks.

Now, from the mantel
I want Neruda in your
knit-pits, scribbling odes

to calves, heels, magic
of arches, love
between toes.

Order This

There's nobody
crossing to snatch
the unopened tall-boy
shimmering on the median
in the passing headlights.

The rock doves scooch
closer together on the arm
of the stoplight
like a harried caterpillar.

Drizzle. Gray sinks
into a body, into tar.
One bird nods off.

A red-tail hawk pins
it to a cloud while
an Amazon Prime van
hauls chicks
to a coop in the city.

Throwback Thursday

Abandoned bike on a path.
Hermes a few yards away
against an oak tree, passed
out.

A toppled
cairn in the distance.

Hanging on the Fridge

Child's sketch of the afterlife
in oblong suns, two-toothed
stick figures, collection
of cursive, mother.

What else survived
when the ranch hand
burned your shed?

The Last Scraps of Sweet and Slow

Crows tear
into the last

doughnut scraps,
this sweet and slow

morning in the Safeway
parking lot. Do they

know my face?
Their caws cupping

my cheeks as I lumber by,
as if grandma has me up

at her eyes, a rush
of cigarettes, whiskey

typing on her teeth after
a night of secretary school.

Kisses

Lovers rejoice.

Those wayward smacks
will land at a county fair
on a mythical pig
named Beatrice,

with eyes that lead
anyone through
troughs of our lives.

Drought

The pond is down twelve feet.
We find the dog's lost tennis balls,
possum and raccoon skulls.

Our skipping stones caught
in the mud-caked cracks,
each year's lost teeth.

Hayfield

Believe me,
there are days

I want to be
the needle

in the haystack,
hayrolls like giant

buttermilk biscuits
drying in the sun.

Dole me out
sparingly in a drought.

Make sure the cattle
proceed field to field

and the tax man gets
his fair flank.

White-Out

Winter's snap
while I walk.

No ATMs around
this white-out scene.

The path spangled, urban legend has it,
with lucky pennies for the plucking,
but I hover

over a buffalo nickel,
a herd thundering
through the valley
of my chest.

Last Frost

It has a way of creeping
in, towels and blankets

shrouding yarrow, false
indigo, oregano. One

night stay, the weight
a pulse as crisp as the first

breath of cold. The temp
in the teens as life stalls

around you—you age
suddenly

as aftermath, as crystal
in the air.

Zero Hour

I'm in my own
birthday parade.

We end
at a church built
on top of a martyr's
index finger.

Entombed
with the relic
a Da Vinci
drawing of an
index finger.

Label: *Here Lies a Holy Touch of
Magnificence.*

It's carnival.

At clean up, I don't
know my job anymore.
This broom, a mask
tangled in the bristles.

Congratulations!

You woke up on a side of the bed,
made it to the scale with a yawn
to swallow digits, blinked
at a fat zero.

Your slack state grazed
the top of that
ballooning oval.

A Buddha emerged,
bellowing laughter,
the number zero painted
on his belly.

He shoved
your jaw closed, brushed
that digit on your torso.

Notes

"White-Out" references a line from Kell Robertson's poem "Song," "Things drop out of our hearts / you could kill a herd of Buffalo with."

"Ode to the Corpse Flower" is for the occasion when said flower bloomed at the Denver Botanical Gardens.

"Stockings" is inspired by Pablo Neruda's "Ode to Socks."

"Congratulations!" is for Jonathan Pierce.

When not teaching at the Community College of Denver, Brian avoids driving as much as possible to connect with quotidian and sacred around him, hang, and shoot hoops. He is also an associate editor of *New Feathers Anthology*. Past publications include two chapbooks, *In a Heart's Rut* (HighFive press), *Maybe This is How Tides Work* (Finishing Line Press), one book, *All Points Radiant* (WordTech, Cherry Grove Editions), and various journals. You can find him on Instragram @brihamwrites.